ESTEBAN VICENTE

AMERINGER

McENERY

YOHE

525 West 22nd Street New York NY 10011

tel 212 445 0051 www.amy-nyc.com

THE INFINITE GARDEN

by Eren Johnson

In an interview with Robert Cordier, Esteban Vicente stated, "I think that no matter what, the painter has to have a sense of the physicality of the world."[1] Following his own directive in his late canvases, Vicente draws from the colors of his native Spain and those cultivated in the garden of his Bridgehampton home. Winnowing a language of forms developed over a lifetime, Vicente merges both color and essential shapes to generate new and unexpected relationships, which celebrate quiet fleeting moments and reinvigorate the quotidian details of time and place with fresh meaning.

As days pass, a habitual blindness to the perceived landscape frequently develops. Routines breed an automatic functioning, as concentration drifts elsewhere. Out of *Spring I* (1996), a newly green landscape rises up, cresting like a wave, seizing attention. Emptied of granular detail, like those found in Vicente's 1938–39 Martha's Vineyard landscapes,[2] the organic is reduced to broad swaths of color. No longer rendered in exacting detail, the pastoral is conveyed by color and raw form alone. What was once specific and defined in Vicente's early landscapes has been removed. The remains emerge as a signifier of place, elemental in form.

1. Esteban Vicente interview with Robert Cordier, undated, Esteban Vicente Archives, EVA 2/407, p.7.
2. Vicente met James Gilbert (American, 1899–1969) in Madrid. The two shared a studio. Gilbert is responsible for introducing Vicente to "plein air" painting. Vicente summered at Gilbert's farm on Martha's Vineyard and maintained a friendship with him until Gilbert's death.

Manifesting form in a primordial state requires a deep-seated understanding of the complex relationships that surround and often mask the form. Observation is primary and imperative. One can rely upon other senses to access and process the physical world, but sight is the only sense by which one can process images. In a critical exchange with a student, Vicente observed, "The head comes after you do something—through the eye."[3] He bestows the signifier primacy over the signified. The eye is the beginning; the idea follows.

To fully comprehend Vicente's privileging of the eye, it is necessary to turn to Spain and his formative years. Seeking better educational opportunities for his children, Vicente's father, Torribio Vicente Ruiz, moved the family from the provincial town of Turégano to Madrid shortly after Vicente's birth in 1903.[4] Educated by the Jesuits, the young Vicente accompanied his father on weekly trips to the Prado museum. The memories of the visits were far from fond; Vicente often recalled the Prado as a "horrible place."[5] Nevertheless, the excursions served as Vicente's first introduction to the masters of European art. Later, he would cite this early exposure to Diego Velázquez, Francisco Goya, and Francisco de Zurbarán as influential. While Vicente would spend a lifetime painting, his first experience of the medium assumed the form of observation.

Four (1996) and *Untitled #6* (1998) savagely reward the eye for looking. Goya's reds are recontextualized. Freed of their subject matter, the fiery reds evolve into pure sensation and atmosphere in Vicente's canvases.

3. *Esteban Vicente: Portrait of an Artist*, directed by Madeline Amgott (2007; internally produced in 2011), DVD, EVA M-146.
4. Elizabeth Frank, *Esteban Vicente* (New York: Hudson Hills, 1995), p.11.
5. Ibid.

Thin veils of yellow and orange stain the canvas in *Four*. The edges of primal shapes bleed into one another. Space between the forms dissolves. Two years later, Vicente revisited the palette of *Four* in *Untitled #6*. Despite the shared palette, the paintings elicit profoundly disparate responses. With subtle adjustments to the saturation of the pigment and attention to the edges in *Untitled #6*, the relationships of the forms emerge dynamic. Rudimentary architectural elements advance in the pictorial space.

Although he later abandoned sculpture as a serious pursuit, Vicente's early academic training in that medium[6] remains crucial to understanding the constructed space in his works. Purging the works of recognizable subjects in the late 1940s, Vicente considered reducing the concrete to the essential to be a fundamental aim of art.[7] Through the 1950s and '60s, Vicente developed a personal language of forms and marks that varied from organic to architectural. These essential elements serve as the building blocks for structuring his pictorial space.

Sculptors are trained to perceive the object's effect on three-dimensional space, as well as the effect of space upon the object. The pictorial space of *Color Luz* (1999) borders on a classical perspectival space. Pink and red vertical slabs of color frame the center of the canvas. A green swath reads as ground. In this completely synthetic space, the eye navigates in and around the slabs as objects. The forms of *Untitled* (1996) provide a rhythmic notation as they puncture the surface of the painting. The blocks of color are defined by the overlaid grey-green paint, while horizontal bands become plinths for

6. Various publications have stated Vicente's matriculation date as 1919, 1920, or 1921 for the Royal Academy of Fine Arts of San Fernando. The staff of the Esteban Vicente Museum of Contemporary Art has carried out new research and established 1918 as the year of Vicente's matriculation. The primary source is the academic registers for the Royal Academy.
7. Esteban Vicente interview with Robert Cordier, undated, Esteban Vicente Archives, EVA 2/409, p.9.

the suspended orange forms. Obscuring the true boundaries of the forms, Vicente alludes to the monumentality of the hidden forms.

Years later, when questioned on the shift from sculpture to painting, Vicente remarked, "the mechanics of a sculptor are so lengthy—in order to reach a point at which you are moved by what is happening."[8]

In comparison to sculpture, painting is immediate. When the painter is alone in the studio, it is solely the brush and pigment that stands between the painter's hand and the realized image. With Vicente's long-held belief in painting as an expedient means to an end, it is a mistake to read his late surfaces as meager or hasty. Rather, they should be taken as painting distilled to its essence. The meaty impasto surfaces of the 1960s have been scraped bare, leaving lean quantities of pigment (only what is necessary to achieve the maximum sensorial effect remains) dispersed on the surfaces.

As Vicente observed, "the reality of painting, after all, is sensuous."[9] *Tact* (1995) excites the eye with its opulent pink ground. A sumptuous red form recedes as it hovers. Simultaneously, the yellow shapes advance and move across the surface. He achieves Hans Hofmann's "push-pull" by constructing space with color. The slivers of bare canvas remain as trace reminders of deliberate moments, brief pauses. These fragments, remnants of process, are evidence of the subtle yet rich layering of Vicente's late canvases.

8. Ibid.
9. Esteban Vicente, "Painting Should Be Poor," *Location* 1, no. 2 (Summer 1964): 69.

The spare surface of *Intuition #2* (1995) exists as hazy veils of blues and greys and obliterated edges. There are intrusions in this fog. Vaguely defined forms frame the edges of the canvas. Dreamlike interruptions of saturated brushwork punctuate the surface, drawing the focus of the eye. At this nexus of mark and veil, nothing is revealed; there is simply a continuation of the mist. Kirk Varnedoe remarks that "in abstract art, we face the particular problem of interpreting images that resemble any number of things, but look like nothing in particular."[10] Guided by Vicente's title, we must reach inward, allowing the painting to draw forth our experiences and memories to establish a responsive dialogue. Meaning unfolds in the transitional space that lies between painting and self.

Vicente, a noted teacher, did not produce volumes of writing about his work or about the work of other artists. He concentrated on his daily studio practice, which is not to say that he lacked definitive views on painting. Taken from an index card in his personal papers, a hastily jotted note reads: "Painting cannot be explained ... intuition is the guide."[11] Vicente requires the observer's participation in acknowledging the gap between an artist's intention and what is in the eye of the beholder.

At the heart of any assessment of Vicente's late paintings lies the response to his emphasis on color, whether it veers toward color field, like *Interval* (1995) and *Composicion* (1998), or toward a structured composition with organic forms, like *Green Floating* (1997) and *Untitled #13* (1997). Vicente concerned himself with the "physical effect of colors not only

10. Kirk Varnedoe, *Pictures of Nothing: Abstract Art Since Pollock* (New Jersey: Princeton University Press, 2006), p. 31.
11. Esteban Vicente, notecard, undated, Esteban Vicente Archives, EVA 3/603.
12. Ibid.

upon the eye, but upon other senses—physical sensation."[12] The ochre and sienna of *Interval* and *Composicion,* the spring greens of *Green Floating* and *Untitled #13* induce a sensation of warmth and pleasure, evoking delight at the opportunity to stand and observe the landscape as the wild colors emerge.

Consciously cultivated by Vicente and his wife, Harriet,[13] the garden, with its riot of colors, often dominates the discussion of Vicente's final works, but it is not singular in its fertility. In the late works, Elizabeth Frank assessed Vicente's task to be "that of finding out how much of what he already knows can lead him to new discoveries, how much can he include without overcrowding, how far can he stretch his vocabulary in new and unexpected directions."[14] The massed and turbulent calligraphic lines of the 1950s dissolve. *On the Way* (1994) no longer depends on an impenetrable wall of marks to solidify its presence. Weightless in its application, the sprayed pink masses provide a counterweight to the ethereal green ground, rendering the totality of the ground inscrutable. Concurrently, the pink block concentrates attention on the few calligraphic marks and the composed space, Vicente's lifelong pursuit.

Executed in Vicente's 96th year, *Ideal Forms* (1999), with its poppy-red shapes layered with pink brushwork, is the continuation of the long dialogue he held with painting and a summation that is poignant in its urgency. A synthesis of forms, brushwork, color, and light, the yellow ochre ground loosely expands, while simultaneously emitting and absorbing

13. Vicente married Harriet Godfrey Peters in 1961. The Bridgehampton home was acquired in 1964.
14. Elizabeth Frank, *Esteban Vicente* (New York: Hudson Hills, 1995), p. 109.

light. With the title, Vicente lays bare his thoughts on what is present in this painting: forms hinted at in his earliest paintings from the 1930s, forms arrived at in the 1950s, forms now emptied to their essence, forms that Vicente revisited and reworked until the last days of his life.

Few artists of Vicente's generation were gifted with his lifespan of investigation. Tragically, Jackson Pollock's, Franz Kline's, and Mark Rothko's explorations were cut short; it has fallen to younger generations of artists to advance their language of painting. Of the artists who persisted, there is a temptation to devalue the late works as less worthy than those from their mature canon. But Willem de Kooning's late canvases, which were challenged in their early reception, are now understood to be "a compacting of his early work" with direct links to sets of forms unbroken from the 1940s to the 1980s.[15]

Similarly, Vicente's late canvases are a testament to his enduring pursuit of abstraction. Aerated forms hover on expanding grounds. Saturated in color and light, the paintings vibrate with an internal order developed over eight decades. It is tempting to draw a straight line through the history of abstraction to some terminal point, some ultimate summation. Vicente's life and art provide evidence to the contrary. Abstraction is not finite. Abstraction is a continued and continuing exploration. ■

Eren Johnson is the Head of the Vicente Archives and Editor of the Esteban Vicente Catalogue Raisonné Project.

15. Kirk Varnedoe, *Pictures of Nothing: Abstract Art Since Pollock* (New Jersey: Princeton University Press, 2006), p. 240.

Tact, 1995
Oil on canvas
29 x 30 inches
73.7 x 76.2 cm

Impulse 2, 1998
Oil on canvas
52 x 42 inches
132.1 x 106.7 cm

Untitled, 1996
Oil on canvas
50 x 42 inches
127 x 106.7 cm

Interval, 1995
Oil on canvas
50 x 42 inches
127 x 106.7 cm

Untitled, 1999
Oil on canvas
52 x 42 inches
132.1 x 106.7 cm

Untitled #10, 1997
Oil on canvas
52 x 42 inches
132.1 x 106.7 cm

Untitled #6, 1998
Oil on canvas
52 x 42 inches
132.1 x 106.7 cm

Green Floating, 1997
Oil on canvas
52 x 42 inches
132.1 x 106.7 cm

On the Way, 1994
Oil on canvas
40 x 32 inches
101.6 x 81.3 cm

Light 2, 1998
Oil on canvas
52 x 42 inches
132.1 x 106.7 cm

Untitled, 1996
Oil on canvas
50 x 42 inches
127 x 106.7 cm

Ideal Forms, 1999
Oil on canvas
52 x 42 inches
132.1 x 106.7 cm

Experience, 1998
Oil on canvas
52 x 42 inches
132.1 x 106.7 cm

Intuition #2, 1995
Oil on canvas
50 x 42 inches
127 x 106.7 cm

Composicion, 1998
Oil on canvas
52 x 42 inches
132.1 x 106.7 cm

Spring I, 1996
Oil on canvas
50 x 42 inches
127 x 106.7 cm

Four, 1996
Oil on canvas
52 x 42 inches
132.1 x 106.7 cm

Untitled #13, 1997
Oil on canvas
52 x 42 inches
132.1 x 106.7 cm

Color Luz, 1999
Oil on canvas
52 x 42 inches
132.1 x 106.7 cm

Untitled, 1995
Oil on canvas
29 x 30 inches
73.7 x 76.2 cm

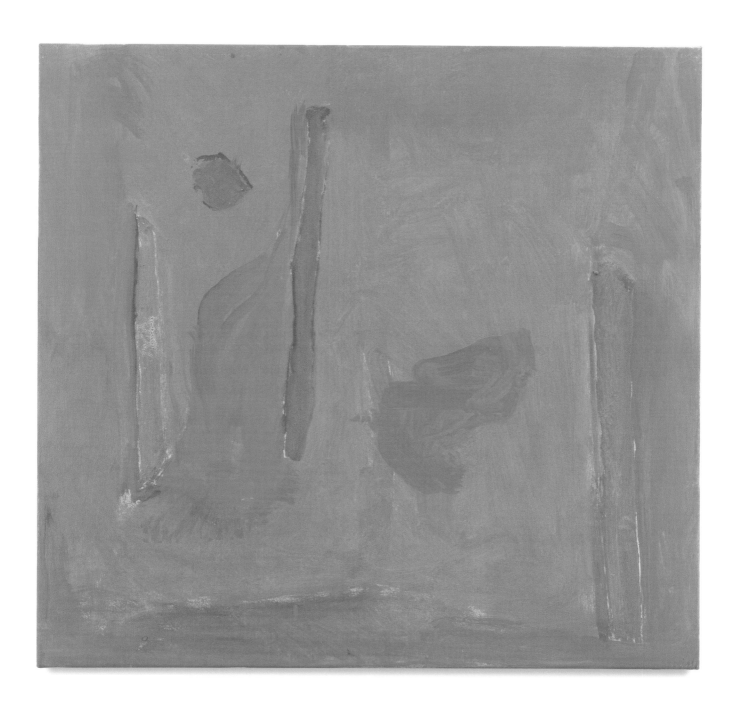

CHRONOLOGY

1903
Esteban Vicente is born on January 20 in Turégano, Spain, in the province of Segovia. He is the third of six children of Toribio Vicente Ruiz and Sofía Pérez y Alvarez. His father, an army officer, is also an amateur painter.

1904-1919
His father resigns from the Civil Guard to take up a post as a property administrator with the Banco de España in order to bring up his children in Madrid. Esteban studies at a Jesuit school. From the age of four, he accompanies his father on visits to the Prado Museum.

1920
Vicente enters the Military Academy but leaves after three months.

1921
Enrolls in the School of Fine Arts of the Real Academia de San Fernando in Madrid at the age of eighteen. He studies sculpture there for three years.

1922-1928
Develops friendships with the poet Juan Ramón Jiménez and members of Generation of 1927, an influential group of poets that included Rafael Alberti, Jorge Guillén, Pedro Salinas and Federico García Lorca. He also befriends the future film director Luis Buñel, the writer and publisher Ernesto Giménez Caballero, and the painters Juan Bonafé, Francisco Bores and Wladyslaw Jahl. He shares a studio on the Calle del Carmen with the American painter James Gilbert; their friendship continues until Gilbert's death in the '70s. He holds his first exhibition in 1928 with Bonafé at the Ateneo de Madrid.

1929
Goes to Paris. Lives in a hotel and later shares a studio with the painter Pedro Flores. Earns a living retouching photographs and working on stage sets at the Folies Bergère.

Visits Picasso at his studio on the rue La Boétie and participates in the Salon des Surindépendants. Meets the young American Michael Sonnabend, who later becomes his art dealer in New York. Spends six months in London, where he visits the painter Augustus Johns and members of his circle.

1930–1934
He moves to Barcelona and through his dealers, Joan Meri and Montse Isern, exhibits at the Galeries Syra. Returns to Paris (1930-31), thanks to a grant from the Junta para la Ampliación de Estudios for study abroad. Meets the Surrealist painter Max Ernst through an English friend, Darcy Japp. Again exhibits in the Salon des Surindépendants. Has one-man shows in Barcelona at Avinyó (1931), Syra (1931), Busquets (1934) and Catalònia (1934). Exhibits in Madrid in the salon of the Heraldo de Madrid (1934).

1935
In Barcelona he marries Estelle Charney (Esther Cherniakofsky Harac), a young American studying at the Sorbonne. They spend a year on the island of Ibiza.

1936
Returns to Madrid in July at the outbreak of the Spanish Civil War. Works at camouflage in the mountains near Madrid before leaving for America. Lives on Minetta Lane, in the Greenwich Village section of New York City.

1937
His daughter Mercedes is born. Thanks to the painter and critic Walter Pach, he has his first solo show in New York at the Kleemann Gallery. At the request of Fernando de los Ríos, the Spanish ambassador to the United States for the Republic, he works at the consulate in Philadelphia until the end of the Spanish Civil War in 1939.

1939
Returns to New York. Has his second individual exhibition at the Kleemann Gallery.

1940
He becomes an American citizen. Lives on Bleeker Street in Greenwich Village.

1941
Participates in a group show at the Pennsylvania Academy of the Fine Arts in Philadelphia.

1942-1945
Teaches Spanish at the Dalton School and works as an announcer for Voice of America during World War II. His daughter, Mercedes, dies in 1943. He divorces Estelle Charney in 1943 and marries the literary critic and educator María Teresa Babín in 1944. Lives at 280 Hicks Street in Brooklyn and works in a studio at 43 Greenwich Street in Greenwich Village.

1945–1946
Teaches painting at the University of Puerto Rico in San Juan.

1947-1948
Returns to New York. Lives and works at 138 Second Avenue. Forms friendships with the painters Willem de Kooning, Jackson Pollock, Mark Rothko, Franz Kline and Barnett Newman and the critics Harold Rosenberg and Thomas B. Hess.

1949
Teaches at the University of California, Berkeley, and begins to work in collage.

1950
Sets up a studio at 88 East 10th Street, which he shares for a time with de Kooning. Chosen by the critic Clement Greenberg and the art historian Meyer Shapiro for the show *Talent 1950* at the Kootz Gallery in New York. Participates in the *Annual* exhibition at the Whitney Museum of American Art. Has a solo show at the Peridot Gallery in New York. Establishes lasting friendships with the painters Balcomb Greene, Aristodemos Kaldis, Elaine de Kooning, Mercedes Matter and Ad Reinhardt, and the sculptors David Hare, Ibram Lassaw, Philip Pavia and George Spaventa.

1951
Helps organize and participates in the historic *9th Street* exhibition. Included in the seminal work on the New York School by Thomas B. Hess, *Abstract Painting: Background and American Phase*. Works daily in his studio and receives visits from Philip Guston, Earl Kerkham, and Landes Leitin, as well as the art collector Ben Heller. Chosen for the first group show of the New York School sent to France and Japan. Named director of summer courses at the Highfield Art School in Falmouth, Mass., on Cape Cod. Teaches painting and organizes shows of Giorgio Cavallon, Willem de Kooning and Kline, among others, in the school gallery.

1953
Elaine de Kooning's article "Vicente Paints a Collage" is published in *Art News*. Vicente has one-man shows at the Allan Frumkin Gallery in Chicago and the California Palace of the Legion of Honor in San Francisco. Teaches during the summer at Black Mountain College in Black Mountain, N.C. Other teachers include the poets Charles Olson and Robert Creeley, the composers Stefan Wolpe and John Cage, and the dancer Merce Cunningham. Among his students is the painter Dorothea Rockburne. He exhibits in several collective shows throughout the United States.

1955
Has solo show at the Charles Egan Gallery in New York, a gallery that also exhibits work by Cavallon, Joseph Cornell, Willem de Kooning, Kline, Reuben Nakian and Jack Tworkov. Participates in several collective exhibitions.

1957
Has one-man show at the André Emmerich Gallery in New York. Accepts a teaching position at New York University, where he remains until 1964. Considered by Harold Rosenberg to be one of the "leaders in creating and disseminating a style…[that] constituted…the first art movement in the United States."

1961
Divorces María Teresa Babín and marries Harriet Godfrey Peters. Lives in the Gramercy Park section of New York.

1962
Awarded a grant from the Tamarind Lithography Workshop in Los Angeles. Teaches at the University of California, Los Angeles, and Yale University.

1964
Founding member of the New York Studio School of Drawing, Painting and Sculpture, together with Mercedes Matter, Charles Cajori and George Spaventa. With his wife, Harriet, buys Dutch colonial farmhouse in Bridgehampton, N.Y. Sets up a studio there and plants a flower garden.

1965
Arist-in-residence at Princeton University, where he has an individual show. Travels to Mexico.

1966
Travels to Morocco.

1967
The death of his friend Ad Reinhardt deeply affects him.

1969
He is artist-in-residence at Honolulu Academy of Fine Arts. Selected to exhibit in *The New American Paintings and Sculpture: The First Generation*, curated by William Rubin at The Museum of Modern Art in New York.

1972
Josh Ashbery writes in *Art News* that Vicente is "widely known and admired as one of the best teachers of painting in America." Moves to West 67th Street. Makes a second trip to Morocco.

1973
Teaches at Columbia University.

1975
He accompanies Harriet on a Jain pilgrimage to India.

1979
Has his first solo show at the Gruenebaum Gallery in New York.

1982
Travels to Turkey with Harriet.

1983
Leaves his studio at 88 East 10th Street for a new one on West 42nd Street in the heart of the theater district.

1984
Receives an honorary doctor of fine arts degree from the Parsons School of Design in New York.

1985
Receives the Saltus Gold Medal from the National Academy of Design of New York and an award from the American Academy and Institute of Arts and Letters as "one of the most gifted painters of the first generation of Abstract Expressionists," with "a sensibility trained in Europe with the express purpose of opening the eyes and ears of Americans to the peculiar beauty around them." Travels to Spain.

1987
Has a major retrospective in Madrid at the Fundación Banco Exterior de España: *Esteban Vicente, Pinturas y Collages, 1925-1985*, and also exhibits at the Yares Gallery in Scottsdale, Ariz. Continues teaching at the New York Studio School of Drawing, Painting and Sculpture and maintains contact with students, artists and friends of all ages.

1988
Receives the Childe Hassam-Eugene Speicher Purchase Award from the American Academy and Institute of Arts and Letters in New York. He exhibits at the Galería Theo in Madrid

and is included in eight group shows, among them *Aspects of Collage, Assemblage and the Found Object in Twentieth-Century Art* at the Solomon R. Guggenheim Museum in New York.

1989
Has a solo show of recent oil paintings and collages at the Berry-Hill Galleries in New York.

1990
Has two one-man shows in Spain. Participates in the exhibition, *Drawing Highlights: Eric Fischl, Roy Lichtenstein, Esteban Vicente*, at the Parrish Art Museum in Southampton, N.Y.

1991
Receives the Gold Medal in the Fine Arts from King Juan Carlos and Queen Sofía at the Prado Museum. Has a street named after him in Turégano, his hometown, in honor of his distinguished career as an artist. Teaches master classes at Parsons School of Design and has six individual showings, including one at the Centro de Exposiciones y Congesos in Zaragoza, Spain, and another at the Galerie Lina Davidov in Paris.

1992
Travels to Spain to attend the opening of a solo show at the Palacio Lozoya in Segovia. Has three one-man shows in the United States: at the Berry-Hill Galleries in New York, the Louis Newman Galleries in Beverly Hills, Calif., and the Guild Hall Museum in East Hampton, N.Y. A selection of his work is chosen for the show *Paths to Discovery: The New York School*, at the Baruch College Gallery in New York. He continues to teach master classes at the New York Studio School and Parsons School of Design.

1993
Elected a member of the American Academy and Institute of Arts and Letters at the age of ninety and awarded an honorary doctorate in fine arts from Long Island University,

Southampton College. Receives a Lifetime Achievement in the Arts Award from the Guild Hall Museum in East Hampton.

1994
His most recent works are shown at the Century Association of New York. Celebrates his ninety-first birthday with an exhibition of his latest works at the New York Studio School of Drawing, Painting and Sculpture in the company of past and present students. Travels to Spain to visit family, among them, his sister María, and attends the opening of his one-man show at the Galería Elvira González in Madrid. *Five Decades of Painting* opens at the Riva Yares Gallery in Santa Fe, N.M.

1995
There is a major retrospective of his collages at the IVAM, Centre Julio González, in Valencia, Spain. Hudson Hills Press publishes the monograph *Esteban Vicente* by Elizabeth Frank. Vicente has exhibitions of recent works at the Riva Yares Gallery in Scottsdale and the Berry-Hill Galleries in New York. The Glenn Horowitz Gallery in East Hampton shows a selection of small collages and unique *divertimentos*.

1996
The exhibition *Esteban Vicente, Collages 1950-1994* travels from Valencia, Spain, to the Patrick and Beatrice Haggerty Museum of Art, Marquette University, Milwaukee. Vicente has solo shows of recent works at the Riva Yares Gallery in Santa Fe and the Galería Elvira González. He returns to Spain with Harriet for a family visit. In the fall, he moves his studio to 1 West 67th Street, next door to his apartment. He abandons the use of the spray gun.

1997
He paints twenty works in three months in his new studio. Receives visits from friends William Maxwell and Susan Crile,

among others. His long-time friend Willem de Kooning dies. Writes an article in de Kooning's honor in the *ABC* (Madrid). Holds exhibitions at The Century Association in New York City, the Riva Yares Gallery in Scottsdale, and Berry-Hill Galleries in New York. Restoration work is begun on the future Museo de Arte Contemporáneo Esteban Vicente, sponsored by the Diputación Provincial de Segovia. The board of trustees of the museum is created and the painter and his wife make a formal donation of 148 works.

1998
The retrospective *Esteban Vicente, Obras de 1950-1998* opens at the Museo Nacional Centro de Arte Reina Sofía in Madrid. The exhibition later travels to Santiago de Compostela (Auditorio de Galicia), Valladolid (Museo de la Pasión and Monasterio de Nuestra Señora del Prado) and Palma de Mallorca (Fundación Pilar I Joan Miró and Casal Solleric). He receives the Premio Castilla-León de las Artes. He attends the opening of the Museo de Arte Contemporáneo Esteban Vicente in Segovia, where a permanent collection of his artwork offers a broad view of his entire career. He continues supervising his students' work at the New York Studio School of Drawing, Painting and Sculpture, where he began teaching in 1964.

1999
At the age of 96, he continues painting every day. Travels to Spain with his wife, Harriet, where they are awarded the Gran Cruz de la Orden Civil de Alfonso X el Sabio for their contribution to art. Vicente is also named "Segoviano del Año" and awarded the Premio Arcale by the city of Salamanca. Has a one-man show at the Riva Yares Gallery in Scottsdale. A permanent room devoted to his works opens at the Museo Nacional Centro de Arte Reina Sofía. All these honors, together with his participation

in several exhibitions, mark the culmination of his recognition as an important figure in twentieth-century Spanish art.

2000
Spends the winter in Bridgehampton rather than New York City for the first time. Does several drawings and sketches. Has one-man shows of drawings and collages at the Galería Elvira González and the Berry-Hill Galleries. The magazine *Reviewny* devotes its *Lifetime Achievement Award* issue (July) to Esteban Vicente. In November, a retrospective exhibition, *Esteban Vicente Esencial*, is held at the Museo de Arte Contemporáneo Esteban Vicente.

2001
On January 11, the artist dies at his home in Bridgehampton, shortly before his ninety-eighth birthday. According to his wishes, his ashes are buried in the garden of his museum in Segovia. His death coincides with the homage that was planned for him earlier by the New York Studio School of Drawing, Painting and Sculpture, of which he was a founding member and teacher for thirty-six years. The book *A Mis Soledades Voy*, consisting of famous Spanish poems illustrated with engravings by Esteban Vicente, is exhibited. The book, which he had worked on until shortly before his death, is also shown at an exhibit in the Museo de Arte Contemporáneo Esteban Vicente with the title *El Color Es la Luz: Esteban Vicente 1999-2000*. Included in the catalog are his writings on art. The show later travels to the Museo de Bellas Artes in Bilbao, Spain, and the Monastery of Nuestra Señora del Prado in Valladolid, Spain. A retrospective of his work is held at the Heckscher Museum of Art in Huntington, N.Y., in September. That same month, an exhibition devoted to various aspects of his work opens at the Monastery of Silos in Burgos, Spain, a space that regularly shows an important selection of major contemporary Spanish art.

SELECT PUBLIC COLLECTIONS

Albright-Knox Art Gallery, Buffalo, New York

Allen Memorial Art Museum, Oberlin College, Ohio

American Academy and Institute of Arts and Letters, New York, New York

Art Institute of Chicago, Illinois

Baltimore Museum of Art, Maryland

Berkeley Art Museum, University of California, Berkeley

Blanton Museum of Art, University of Texas at Austin

Broad Art Center, University of California, Los Angeles

Broad Art Museum, Michigan State University, East Lansing

Brooklyn Museum, New York

Brunnier Art Museum, Iowa State University, Ames

The Butler Institute of American Art, Youngstown, Ohio

The Carl Van Vechten Museum, Fisk University, Nashville, Tennessee

Corcoran Gallery of Art, Washington, D.C.

Dallas Museum of Art, Texas

Delaware Art Museum, Wilmington

Detroit Intitute of Arts, Michigan

Fogg Art Museum, Harvard University, Cambridge, Massachusetts

Grey Art Gallery, New York University, New York

Guild Hall, East Hampton, New York

Herbert F. Johnson Museum of Art, Cornell University, Ithaca, New York

Hirshhorn Museum and Sculpture Garden, Smithsonian Institution, Washington, D.C.

Honolulu Academy of Arts, Hawaii

Hood Museum of Art, Dartmouth College, Hanover, New Hampshire

Housatonic Community College, New York

Hudson River Museum, Yonkers, New York

Institut Valenciá d'Art Moderne, Centre Julio González, Valencia, Spain

Los Angeles County Museum of Art, California

Memorial Art Gallery, University of Rochester, New York

The Metropolitan Museum of Art, New York, New York

Museo Colecciones del Instituto de Crédito Oficial, Madrid, Spain

Museo de Arte Contemporáneo Esteban Vicente, Segovia, Spain

Museo de Bellas Artes de Bilbao, Spain

Museo Nacional Centro de Arte Reina Sofía, Madrid, Spain

Museo Patio Herreriano de Arte Contemporáneo Español, Valladolid, Spain

Museum of Contemporary Art, Chicago, Illinois

Museum of Fine Arts, Boston, Massachusetts

The Museum of Modern Art, New York, New York

National Academy Museum, New York, New York

National Gallery of Australia, Canberra

Nelson-Atkins Museum of Art, Kansas City, Missouri

Neuberger Museum of Art, State University of New York, Purchase

Newark Museum, New Jersey

New Jersey State Museum, Trenton

Palm Springs Art Museum, California

Parrish Art Museum, Southampton, New York

Patrimonio Nacional, Spain

Princeton University Art Museum, New Jersey

The Rose Art Museum, Brandeis University, Waltham, Massachusetts

San Francisco Museum of Modern Art, California

Smith College Museum of Art, Northampton, Massachusetts

Smithsonian American Art Museum, Washington, D.C.

Solomon R. Guggenheim Museum, New York, New York

Syracuse University Art Galleries, New York

Tucson Museum of Art, Arizona

University of New Mexico Art Museum, Albuquerque

The Wadsworth Atheneum Museum of Art, Hartford, Connecticut

Walker Art Center, Minneapolis, Minnesota

Weatherspoon Art Museum, University of North Carolina, Greensboro

Whitney Museum of American Art, New York, New York

Williams College Museum of Art, Williamstown, Massachusetts

Worcester Art Museum, Worcester, Massachusetts

Yale University Art Gallery, New Haven, Connecticut

Published on the occasion of the exhibition

ESTEBAN VICENTE

21 April – 21 May 2016

Ameringer | McEnery | Yohe
525 West 22nd Street
New York, NY 10011
tel 212 445 0051
www.amy-nyc.com

Photography by
Christopher Burke Studios, New York, NY

Catalogue designed by
HHA Design, New York, NY

ISBN: 978-1-4951-3015-1

Cover: *Untitled* (detail), 1991, Oil on canvas, 36 x 50 inches, 91.4 x 127 cm

AMERINGER
McENERY
YOHE